A MACDONALD BOOK

First published in Great Britain in 1989
by Macdonald & Company (Publishers) Ltd
London & Sydney
A member of Maxwell Pergamon Publishing Corporation plc.

Printed and bound in Great Britain by
Purnell Book Production Ltd
A member of BPCC plc

Main text set in 16pt Bembo Educational by Goodfellow & Egan Ltd

Macdonald & Co (Publishers) Ltd
66-73 Shoe Lane
London EC4P 4AB

British Library Cataloguing in Publication Data
Linton, Margaret, *1927–*
Hello butterflies.
1. Butterflies
I. Title II. Terry, Trevor III. Series
595.78'9

ISBN 0–356–13886–0
ISBN 0–356–13887–9 Pbk

• NATURE TALES •

• HELLO BUTTERFLIES! •

Written by Margaret Linton and Trevor Terry
Illustrated by Tricia Newell

Macdonald

Once there were three caterpillars.

The first caterpillar was brown with two yellow stripes. It lived on a prickly thistle which was growing at the edge of the buttercup meadow.

It was a very hungry caterpillar and it liked eating thistle leaves.

The second caterpillar was black and very spiky. It lived on a stinging nettle which was growing in a patch beside the farmyard gate.

It was a very hungry caterpillar and it liked eating nettle leaves.

The third caterpillar was green and rather small. It lived in a cabbage which was growing at the bottom of the garden.

Although it was small, it too was a very hungry caterpillar. It liked eating cabbage leaves and it ate and ate. After a while it began to feel tired.

Soon the green caterpillar felt so tired that it decided to have a rest. It crawled to the garden fence and fastened itself under a rail. Then it made itself a little case to rest in.

Outside, everything was quiet and still, but inside the case something wonderful was happening.

One day, the case began to split open. Very slowly, out came – not a green caterpillar – but a small butterfly. She had white wings with black spots on them and her name was Small White.

For a little while she stayed quite still in the warm sunshine. Then she opened her wings and flew to a nearby flower.

Small White flew from flower to flower. She saw the garden, the buttercup meadow and the nettle patch by the farmyard gate.

"I can go anywhere now," she thought. "I'll go and see what has happened to some other caterpillars."

First she flew to the prickly thistle at the edge of the buttercup meadow.

When she got there, Small White had a big surprise. She saw a beautiful butterfly called Painted Lady. She had come from the brown caterpillar with the yellow stripes.

"That's a beautiful butterfly," thought Small White, "but when Painted Lady was a caterpillar, she had to eat thistles. I'm glad I'm me."

And off she flew to the nettle patch.

At the nettle patch, Small White had another surprise. She saw a beautiful butterfly called Red Admiral. He had come from the black spiky caterpillar.

"That's a beautiful butterfly," she thought, "but when Red Admiral was a caterpillar, he had to eat nettles. I'm glad I'm me."

"Now I think I'll fly back to the garden and look for some friends."

Back in the garden, Small White saw a Buddleia bush. All kinds of butterflies were feeding on the juice from its flowers.

"Fancy that!" she thought. "Caterpillars live on different kinds of plants and eat different kinds of food, but all butterflies seem to like this bush. These butterflies can be my friends."

"Hello butterflies!"

hogweed

buttercups

clover

rabbit

magpie

dandelions

dog daisies

spider in web

ladybird

sparrow

grass

bee